JUNGLE MONKEY

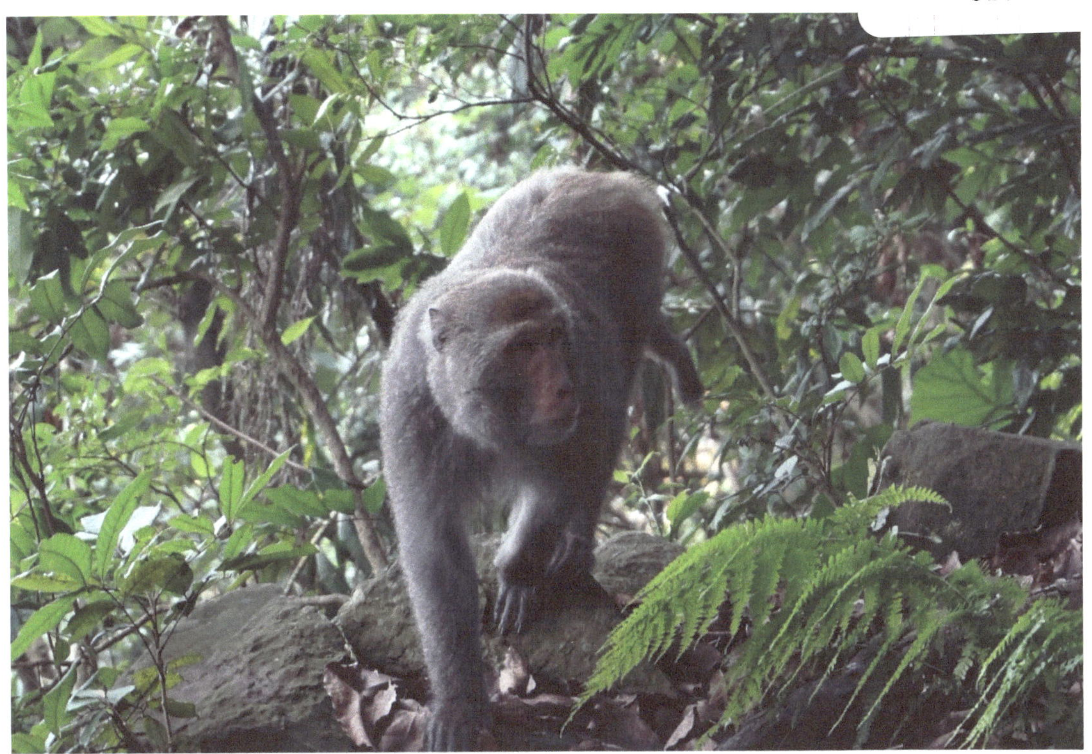

AMOS KING

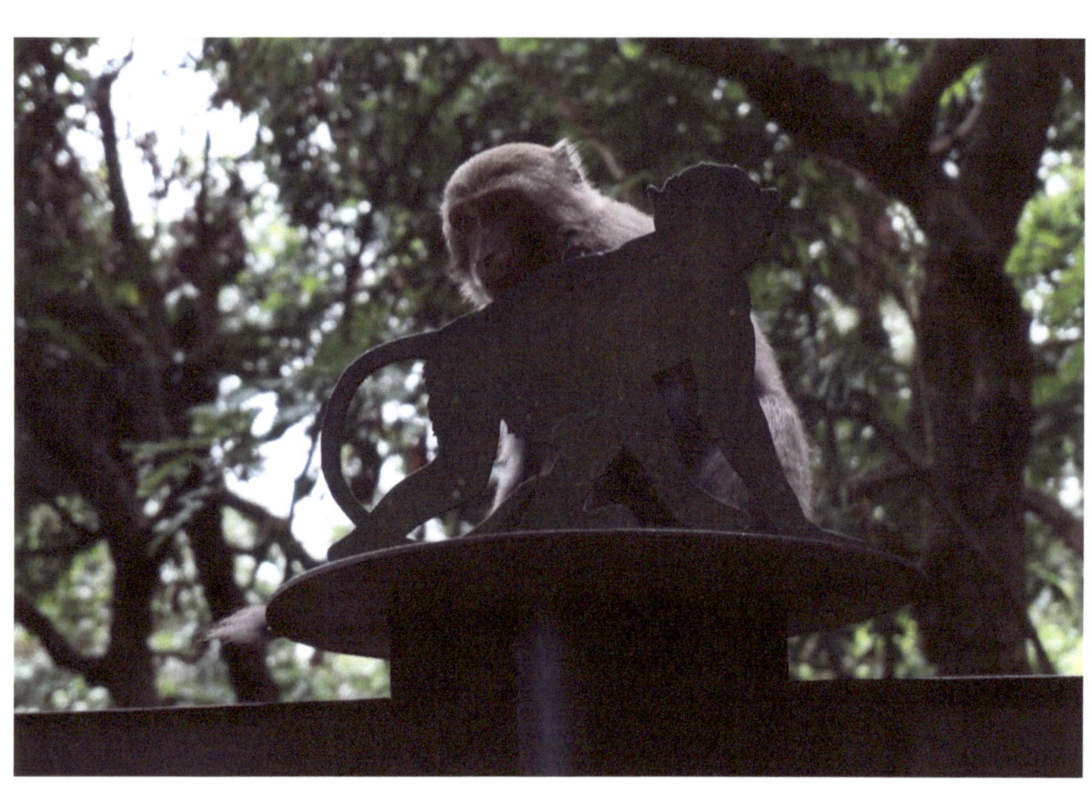

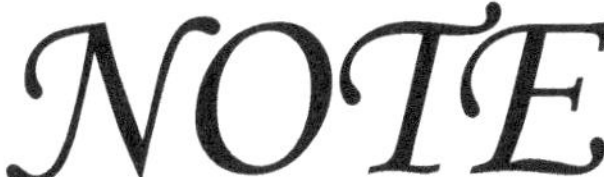

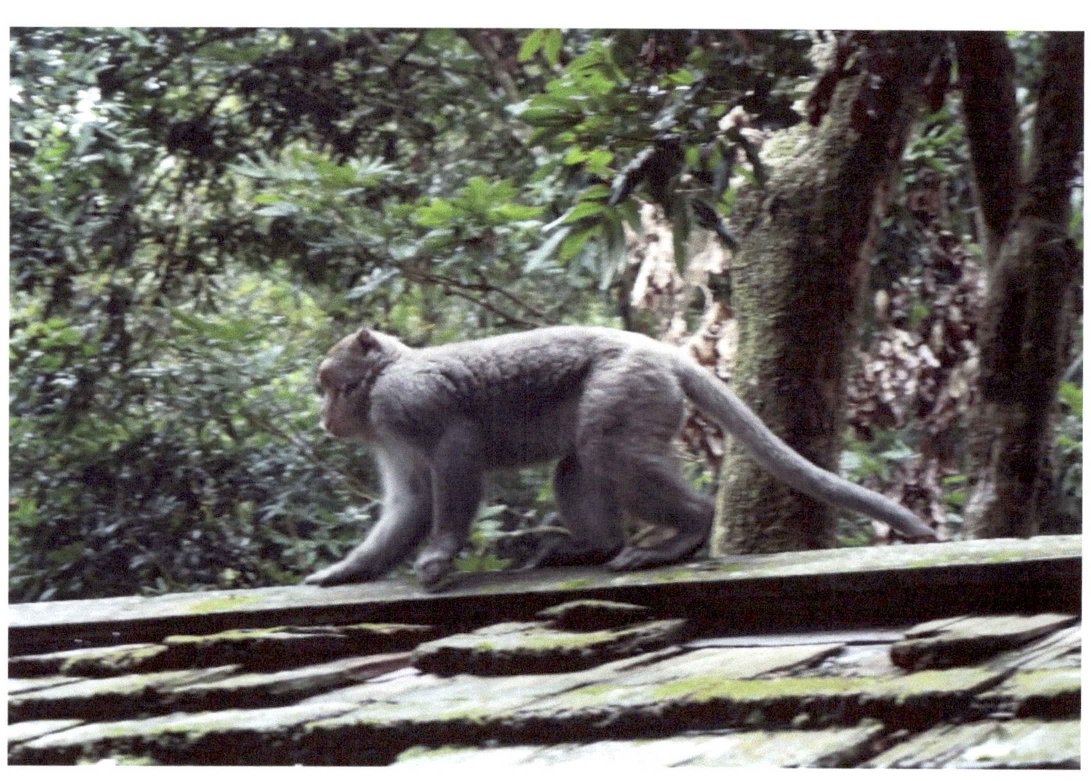

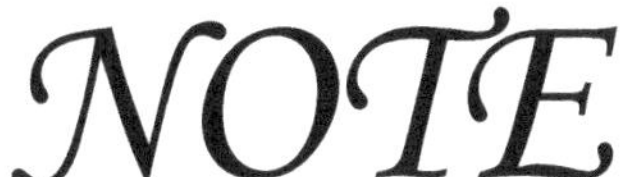

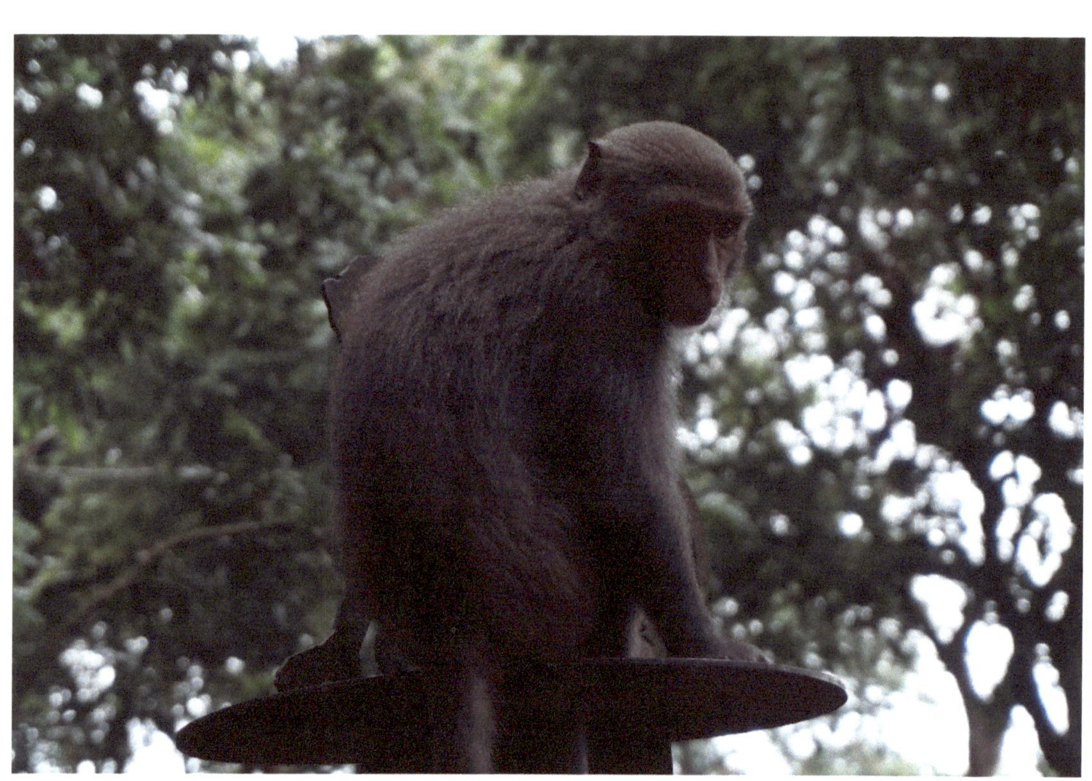

NOTE

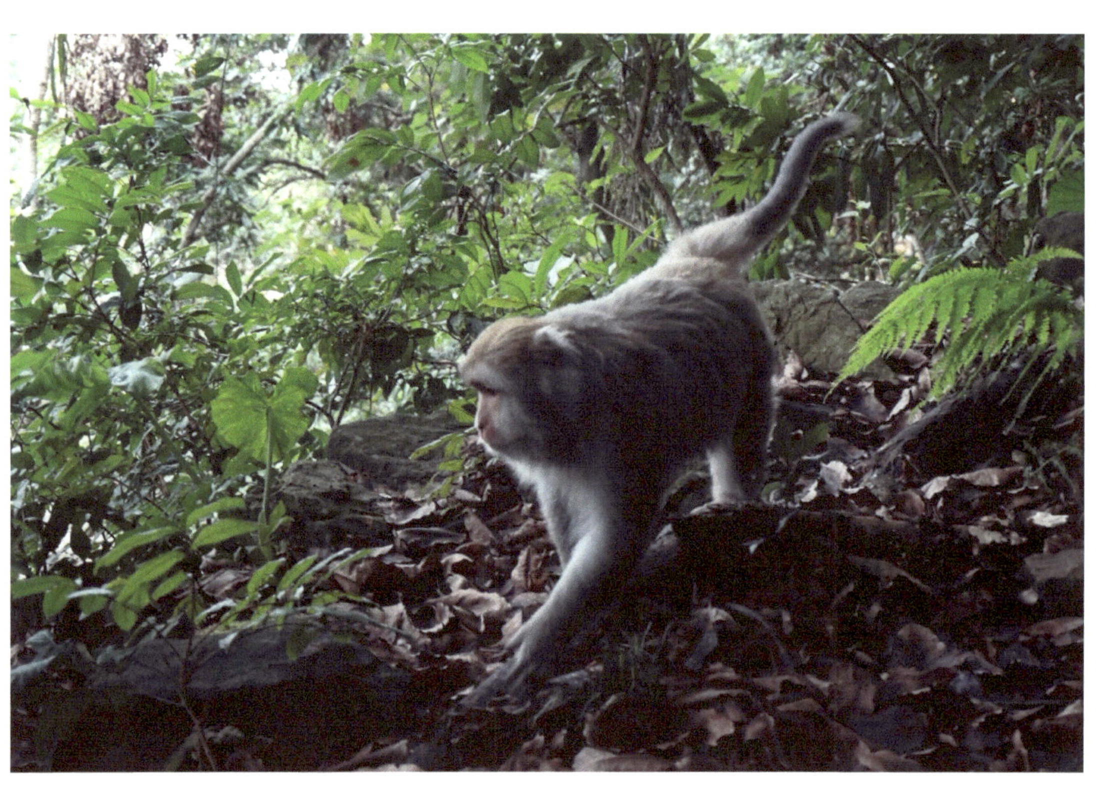

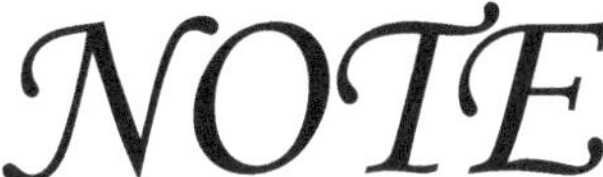

NOTE

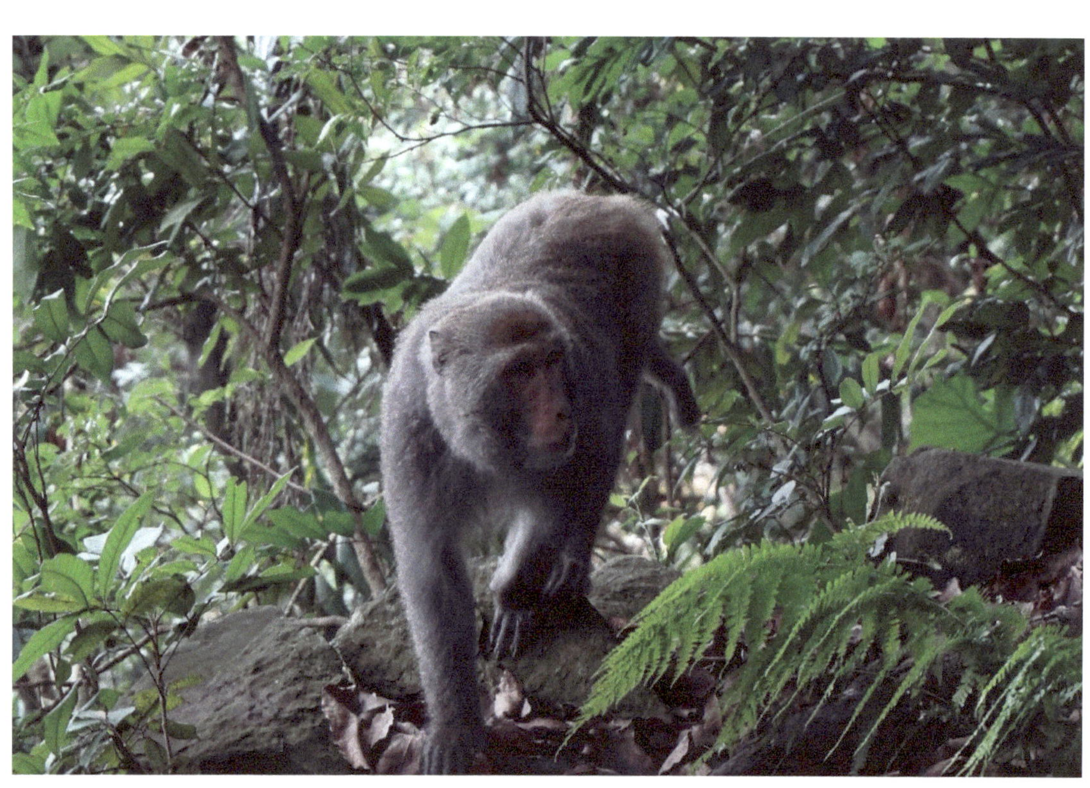

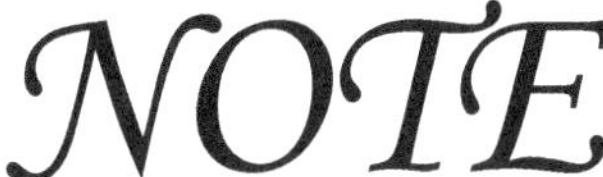

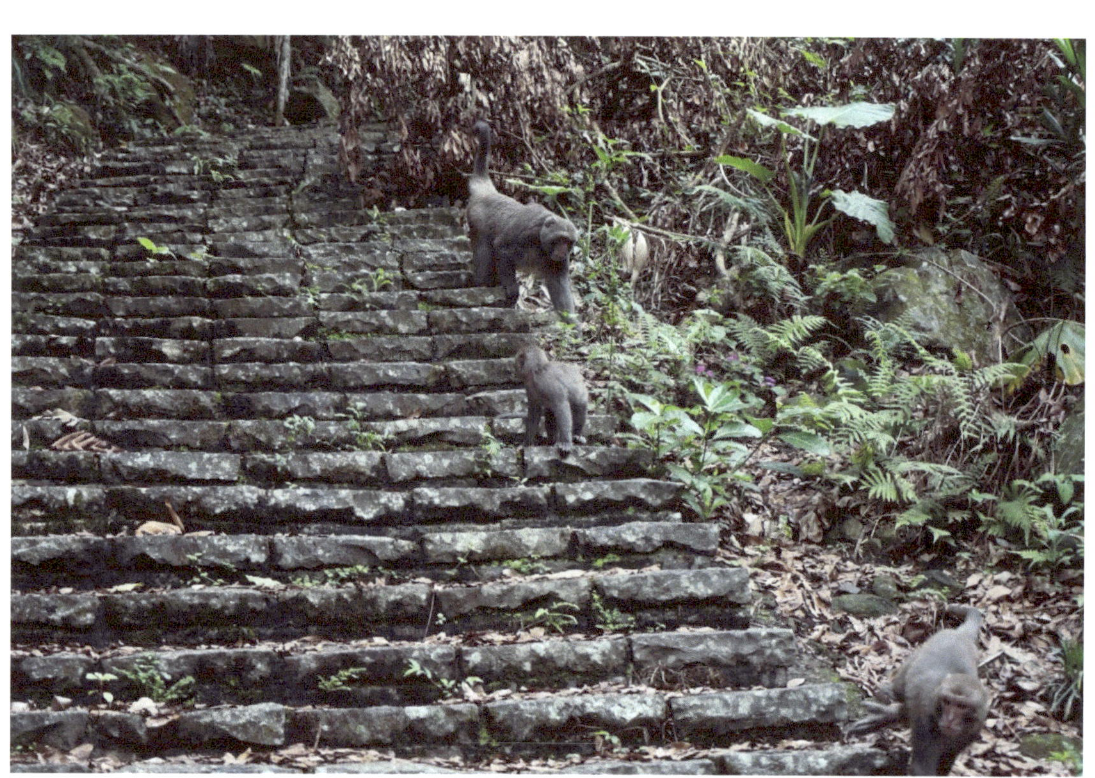

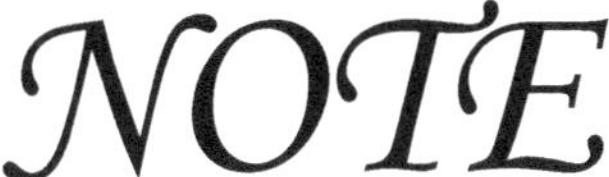

NOTE

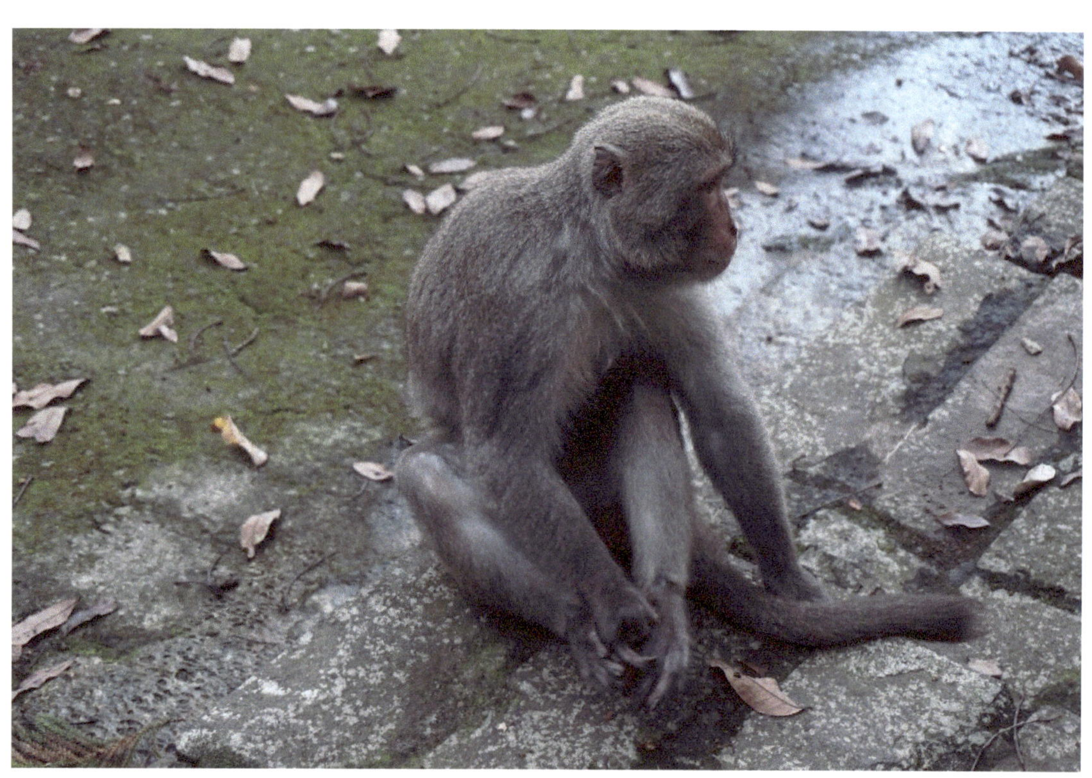

NOTE

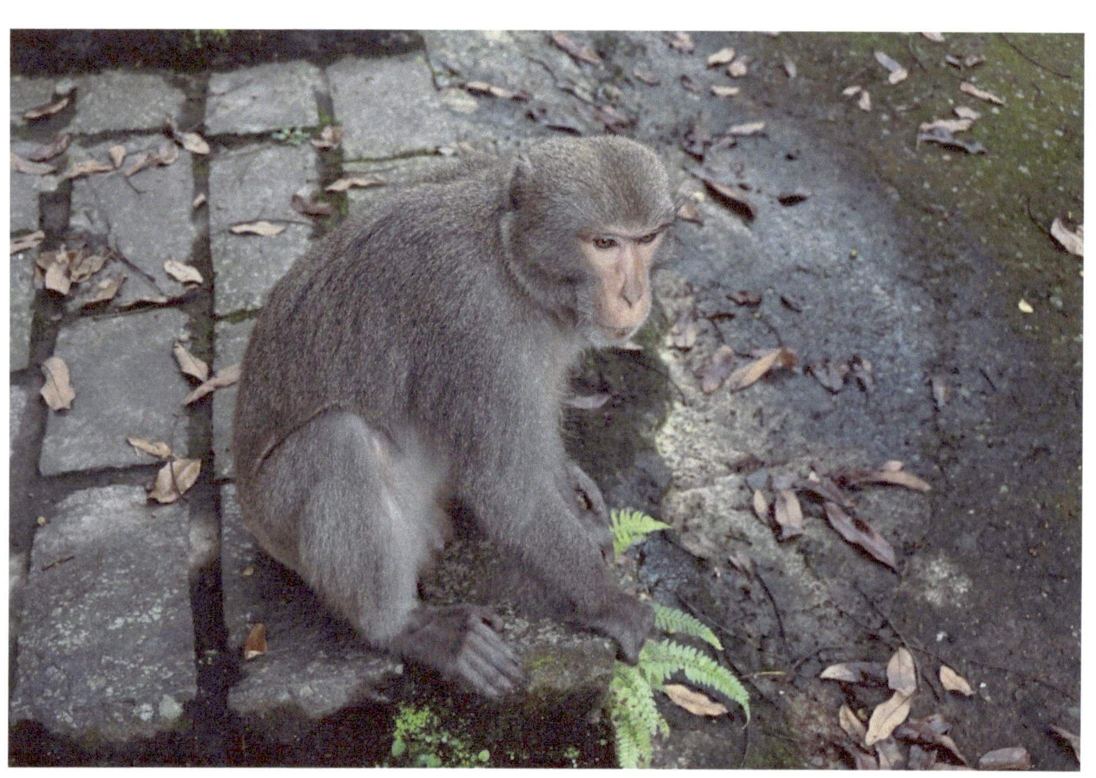

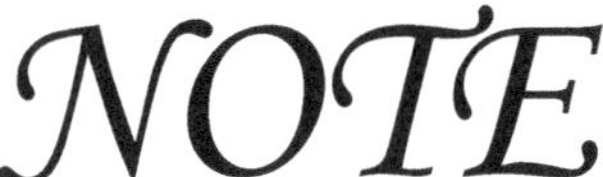

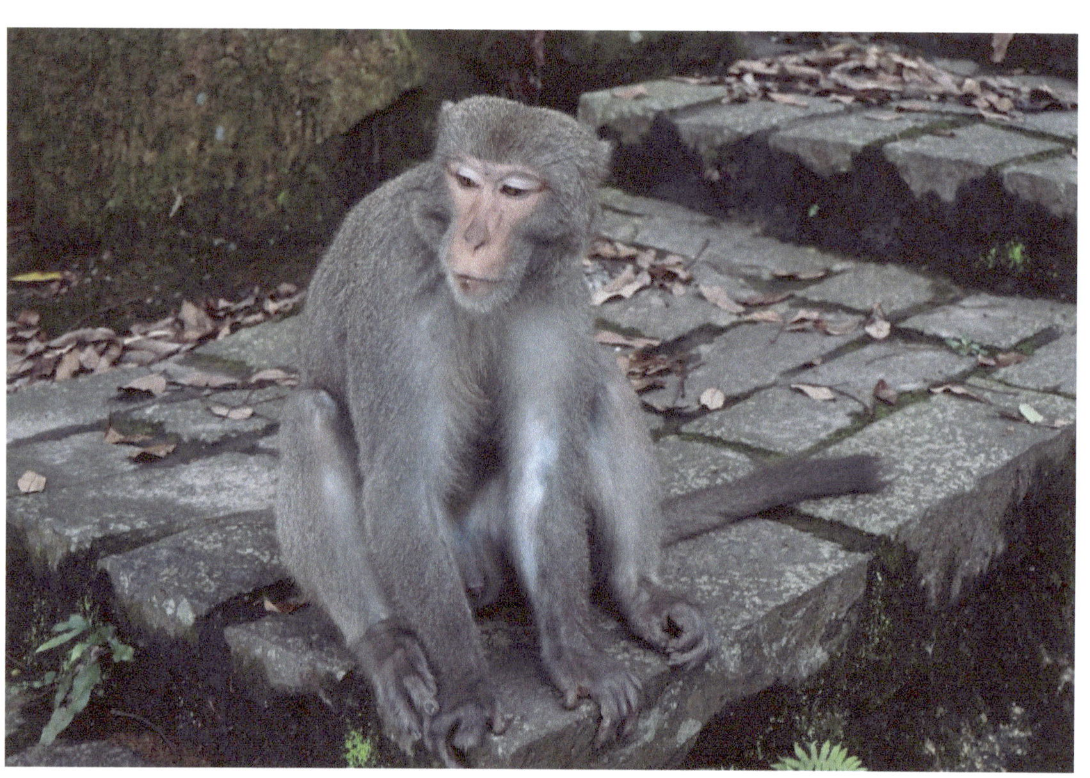

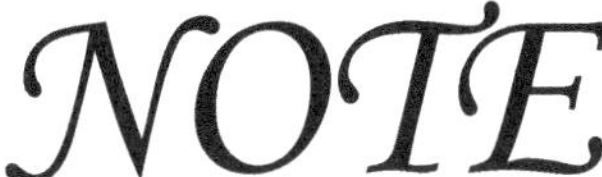

NOTE

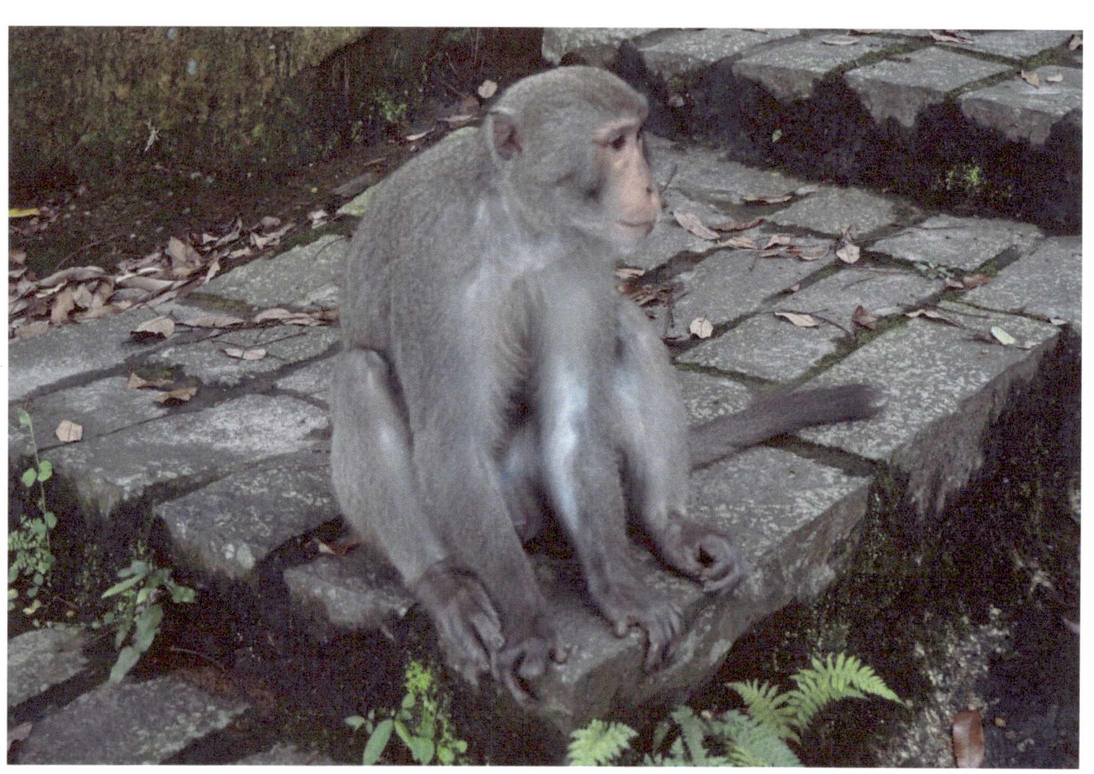

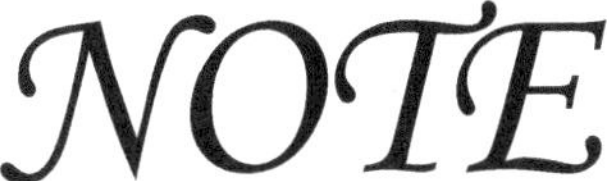

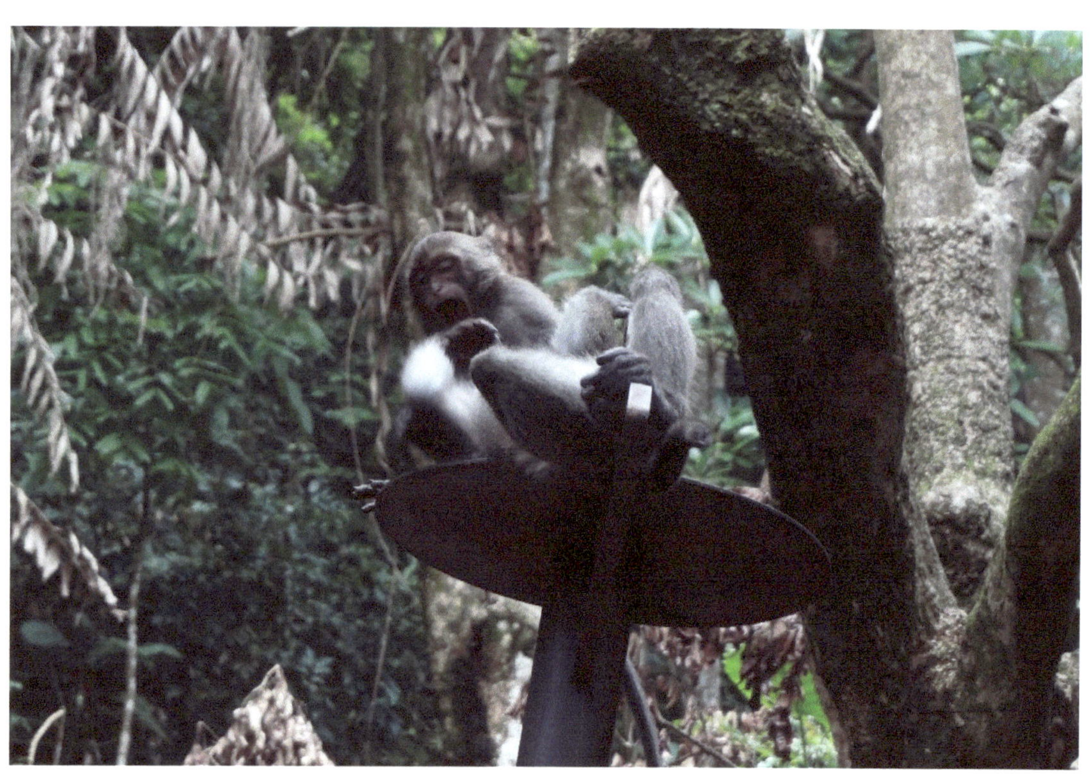

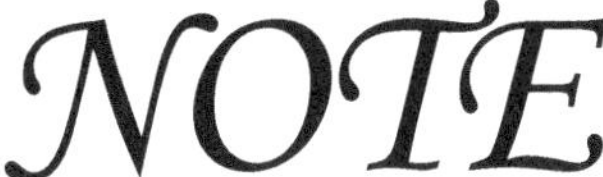

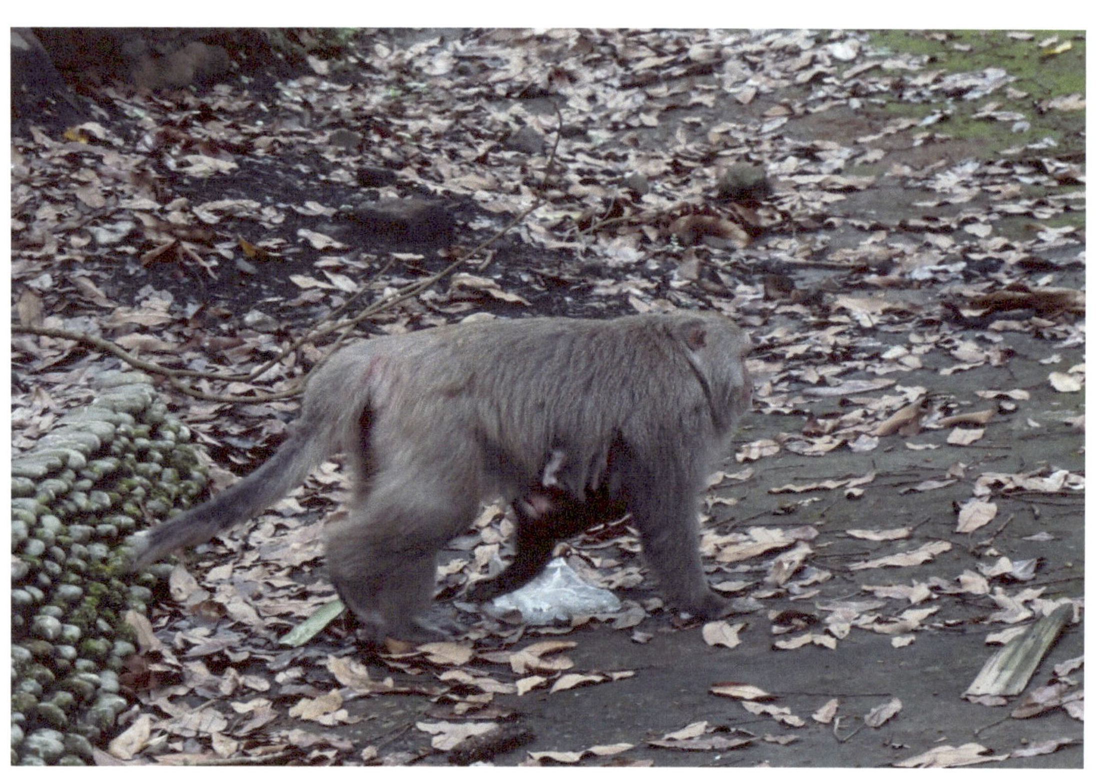

NOTE

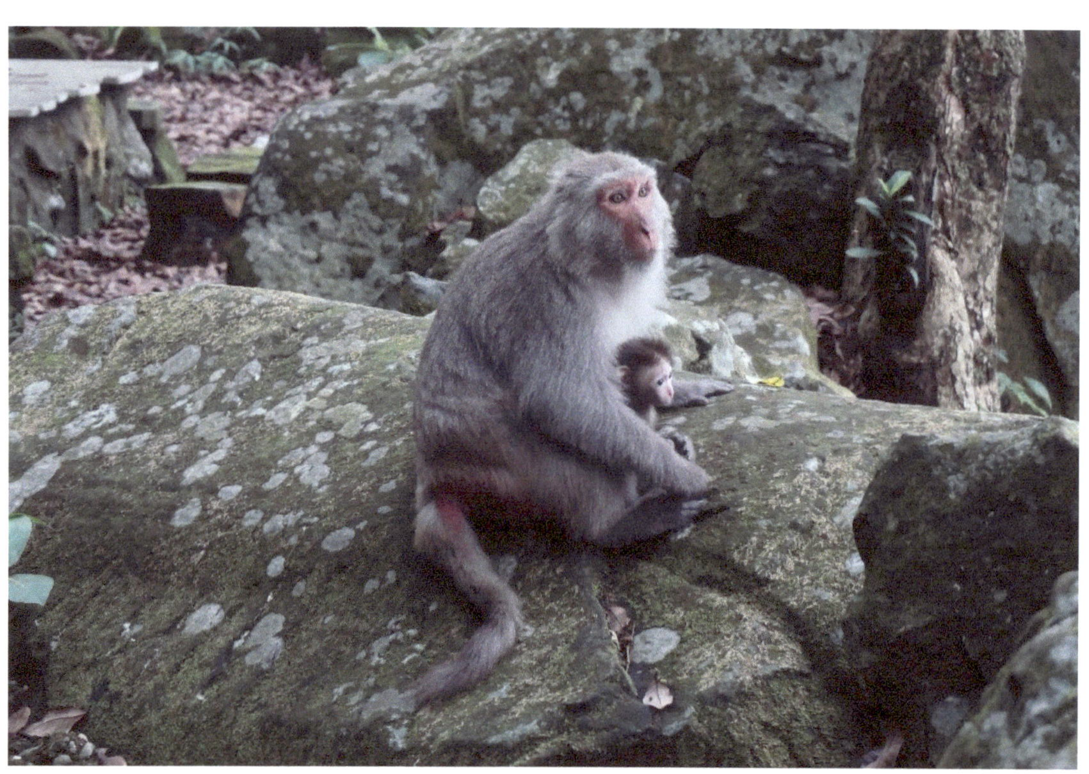

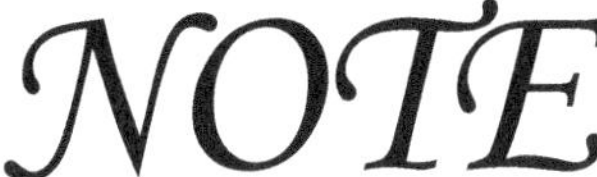

END

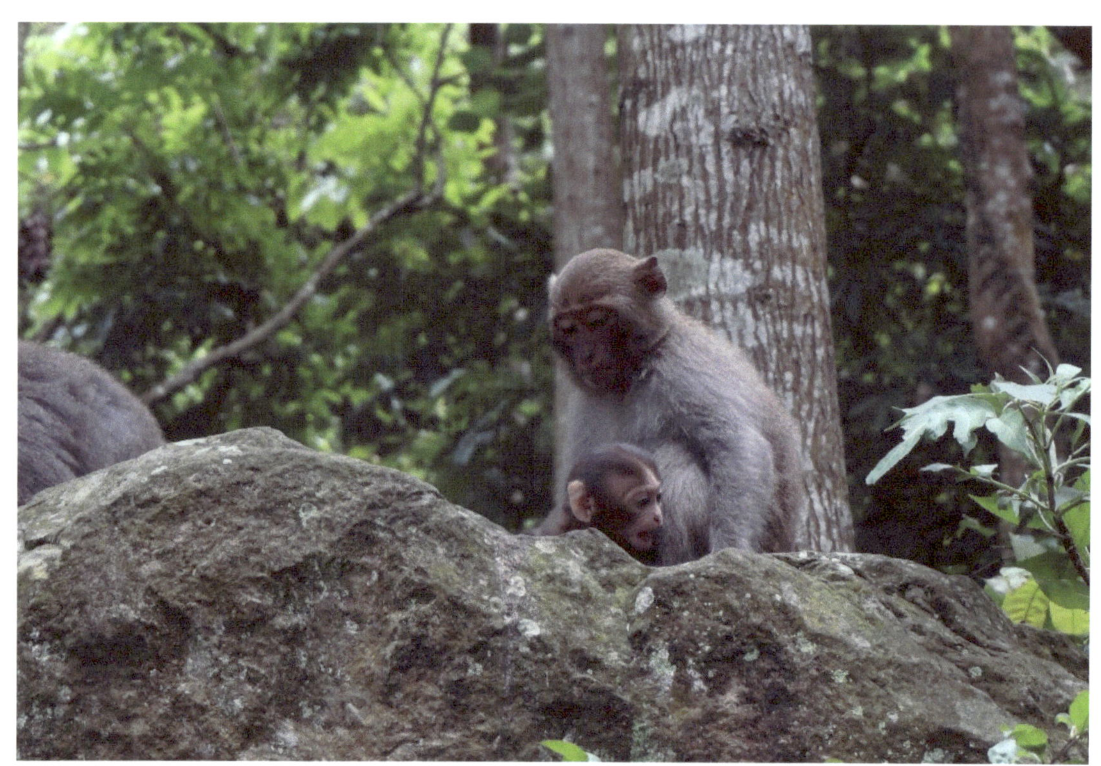